It Was Not Right to Love Him So Much

poems by

Sondra Melzer

Finishing Line Press
Georgetown, Kentucky

It Was Not Right
to Love Him So Much

Copyright © 2023 by Sondra Melzer
ISBN 979-8-88838-157-1 First Edition
All rights reserved under International and Pan-American Copyright Conventions.
No part of this book may be reproduced in any manner whatsoever without written
permission from the publisher, except in the case of brief quotations embodied in
critical articles and reviews.

ACKNOWLEDGMENTS

"A Mermaid's Song" was previous published in National Council of Teachers
of English, *Women in Literacy and Life Assembly,* Volume 1, 1992

Publisher: Leah Huete de Maines
Editor: Christen Kincaid
Cover Art: Barbara Aronica-Buck
Author Photo: Frank Melzer
Cover Design: Elizabeth Maines McCleavy

Order online: www.finishinglinepress.com
also available on amazon.com

Author inquiries and mail orders:
Finishing Line Press
PO Box 1626
Georgetown, Kentucky 40324
USA

Table of Contents

The Mermaid's Song 1

The Green Chair 4

The Red Wall 7

Women's Talk 10

Today's Lesson 12

Reflections on a Running Back 13

About Teaching 14

It Was Not Right to Love Him So Much 18

Her Lover's Landscape 23

For Melissa 26

Always, to Frank
To Melissa, Who Inspires My Life

The Mermaid's Song

It must be told
It must be told
And so it is...
Unspoken words
A heart carries
Inside itself.
Too heavy to bear,
Too hard to say
But there,
Telling its story
Every day
To a life that can't stop listening
To the sounds of the past
Saying to the present
It must be told—
It must be told...

Little girls listen to their heartbeats,
As their fingers fondle the brush ends of their braids
Roped tightly together
Bound by brown rubber bands
Doubled over thick clumps of hair falling gracelessly
Over bent shoulder blades.
They listen to the heavy breathing
Of a whiskey-sodden father
And smell the stench of a man who hated
Himself.

They feel the nights
Descending with the
Menace of the dark;
Unforgiving nights
That keep the secrets of the house,
Till daylight gives them away
To everyone—to everyone—to everyone.

And when they all know
And they will,
Little girls must hide
Or turn inside themselves
To flowing ivory dresses,
Silver-handled mirrors at rest
On soft linen lace,
And yellow roses in cut-crystal vases
That catch the corners of the sun,
Spilling its light
Across pianos
Lacquered bright,
In empty, gorgeous rooms
Of colored-carpeting,
Polished floors,
French doors,
And bound books,
Fitted in shelves that rise
To pale blue mouldings
Framing the beloved space.

Then little girls must see the blanket
Pulled across the mother's face—
Muted rage in every breath
That heaves beneath
The faded quilt
Now worn and used
Like the life
That clutches
To its dingy pattern.

And when the heartbeats stop,
A moment's pause in its
Unrelenting history,
The fingers fall

From the blunted ends of hair
And rise to flooded eyes
To clear the mist ...

And little girls must listen once again.

The Green Chair

There was a big green chair
In the living room
It had big rounded arms
Most of it torn up
But it was his first place to sit.
I hated both of them—then

When he drunkenly
Stumbled toward it
I had to help him up
So he wouldn't fall
On the floor

Those moments
Were the worst
I couldn't let him fall
Too Big
Too drunk—

I could see that green chair
I could see it now
Torn and ripped
Like us
Tired, like us
From overuse

But we would
Puff it up every Saturday
Saturday was cleaning day

And payday at the gas station
And that money, all of it
All of it was handed out
In drunken shows
As he threw them
To every taker

Who knew the ways
Of the drunken fool
Who made a show
Every Saturday—
This inebriated
Side Show.

"Big Shot"
He called himself
And threw more down
Top of the Bar

He smelled of liquor
Chubby hands, bloated face
His watery eyes

Even the wrinkled bills
The wrinkled bills
They were always wrinkled
Wrinkled and wet
I never knew why

The crowds in the bars loved him
This generous drunk
Who threw new bills
In the air

And did a drunken dance
That often ended
When he fell down
And hit his reddened nose

Time to go home,
Stumble up the stairs
Lunge against the door
Find the big Green Chair
Sleep the drunken sleep
Till morning light

Rub the bleary eyes
He lifted himself
Grumpy from the struggle
Of it
Pushed himself up and
Out of it—
Out of the Green Chair

Till next Saturday
When he could
Do his drunken dance
And sleep his drunken sleep
in the big Green Chair.

The Red Wall

"Don't go there," she said
But I always did.
I slid the bolt to the left.
I knew how to do it.
Easy…A practiced skill—
My hand shook
But I knew how to do it.
Just slide the bolt to the left
And there he was.
He pushed his drunken body
Against the door
And he was in.
His eyes red and blotted
From liquor…always the same.
"Get out of here," my mother screamed—
"You don't belong here."
She was right but too late.
We knew the drill,
All his money gone
Wrinkled bills thrown across the filthy bars
He haunted—loved to do it.

All his money is gone. Tens. Fives. Ones.
It made no difference when he got there.
Gone is gone—all gone as he paid Sal the cab
Driver who was waiting outside—
Loyal—an old ritual.
Dropped him off—watched him stumble up
The fourteen stairs—I know it was fourteen
Sometimes I pulled him up myself…I wanted him in…
I wanted him out…I don't know why.
But I know it was fourteen.

Unsteady and smelling of liquor
This night he headed up those fourteen steps
We could not stop him
He was too big
We were too small.

My mother stood in front of me
Again "Get out!" so all the neighbors
Shook their heads and pulled the shades down.
It was a familiar show to them…
"Mack went off again…" Enough said.

You will not hurt us.
You cannot hurt us anymore.

But She was wrong this time.
He saw the ketchup bottle…too late.
He threw it at her head
Blood spurted out.
I know it!
I saw it!
He flung the bottle at her head,
She ducked—I saw it
She ducked—I saw it
It hit her head
Red, Red Everywhere Red
She is dead!
Red, Red, Everywhere Red
The Red sauce dripped down
She was dead

I closed my eyes
He killed her
She was dead.

But no, she was not dead.
The sauce dripped and dripped
And she moaned quietly…sad and exhausted
But she was not dead.
That's all that mattered.

I sobbed and sobbed
And he shuffled past us
But no, he could not kill us
Not then, not ever.

We took some old rags
And scrubbed and scrubbed
The red wall.
But it would not come off.
Silently we scrubbed
But it would not come off.

We scrubbed and scrubbed
Too painful to describe.
We scrubbed and scrubbed
But no matter how we scrubbed

It would not come off—

Sometimes I put my hand to my heart—
It's still there

It never came off. It's still there,
I know it.

Women's Talk

The two of them stood
There in the empty room

A woman's secret had passed between them.

They held their hands over
Their mouths
The way women do
When they whisper
Private female things
To one another.

Titillated with excitement
They reached out—
Hugged each other—
Half laughing, half in despair
Bodies touched
To seal the story now unfolded.

There was something about it—
The way the one had told
About the life she held
So briefly;
At a time when such conception
Should not be.

And the way the other listened,
Amazed and touched,
The details of the bloody business,
The shrunken cord, the shriveled flesh,
That died before its birth.

It was not sad,
For this was a life
Not meant to be.

And right—we all know,
That such a life did not
Come to pass.

But it was amazing still,
The two women, that is.
Standing astride mid-life themselves,

Speaking of birth and bearing
When such talk belongs to youth.

And it was a grand moment, too.
A reminder of the insistence of life
To renew itself,
And to deny itself
When nature says unfit.

And grander still
That two (She and He)
At this more gentle time
Could couple with such passion
To beget another
Heartbeat between them…
Even for so short a time.
So, they stood there,
The two grown women,
Mature and wizened by more
Than half a century of living each,
But young for just a moment,
In the warmth of the afternoon,
Talking women's talk,
Of children born and unborn
(Only women know)
Until it grew late
And they parted, hurriedly,
From each other
To go about the
Women's work
That still needed to be done.

Today's Lesson

We pass through these corridors of time and place
Knowing that this multi-layered city,
Teeming with life—

        Tense and strained
Piercing the woods and rocks of another time and place
Growing in every direction (sometimes all at once)
Pulling from its strong New England roots
And mingling past heritage with present purposes;
An exquisite anachronism,
Stretching astride a pulsating metropolis
               and a rustic expanse of puritan ground—

And We spawn from this soil and out of this city
A generation of the young;
Proud and diverse,
Wise and well taught,
Who bravely undertake the conglomerate world ahead—
As their next assignment.

Reflections on a Running-Back
For Willie

I wonder what happened to Willie.

Do you remember the time
we talked our hearts out in the parking lot—
You astride the battered bike, your bare black chest
Sweating in the killing sun?

Your arm was a track of ragged stitches,
The remnants of a nine-yard run, you said,
As you fought to be free on a field that loved you,
Twisting, pulling, head tucked. Shoulders low.

"No arms around me, no way!
Man, don't pull me down, you Mothers,
I'm Willie…" then crack!

Broken and repaired,
A long terrible scar that worked its way down
The belligerent muscle,
Ugly, unavoidable.
I touched it,
The way I had touched your shoulder
the first day I saw you,
Bad, Willie.

It hurt the tips of my fingers
And broke my heart a little,
And we both knew that the broken limb
Would heal and flex again
But never to reach for the stars
We both had dreamed about.

Did you dream other dreams, Willie?

Come tell me sometime, Willie,
So we can touch again.

About Teaching

I never knew
I wanted to teach
Until I did it.

There is something
About doing something
Not knowing if that's
The something
You always wanted
Always loved.

For how should we
Know that it's
What we always wanted
Always loved

That something lived in our hearts
Untouched—untouchable
Waiting—longing to
Be touched
But not ready—

How do we know
Silly girl—silly
Silly girl

You aspire to great things
A life of importance
In this mundane world

And this—such an unimportant life
For you—oh no!
I must have more

And so you seek—
There must be a life
Of importance—of brilliance
Of joy and fame.

Not empty, sad young faces
Staring at you every day
How pathetic, you think—
I must have more.

How ordinary you are
Certain of that.

To teach—to breathe life
Into those empty faces
Or waiting bodies

Sitting, standing
As if you had such power.
Silly person—there is no way
You are wrong.

To step in front of
Those who wait
And teach!

You have no magic wand
You will never awaken
Those dreary bodies
Or even the brilliant souls
Who have been waiting for you
To teach.

Never, never
Life is not like that
But you are wrong again—
You do not know that yet

You are wrong.
Dear God, you are so wrong.

To teach—to give all
You have—all you know
You didn't think
It would be like this.

It fills you up to
Give so much

But it is like that
You give everything
You have

No—you'll never know it

Till you do it
To teach so they may learn

Whatever it is in your small
Sacred classroom.
You shut the door
And so it begins

Be ready for it
It will take you by storm.

Our dingy sometimes
Glorious rooms
That you fill up with yourself
And your students

A public-private spectacle
Just you and them.
But you don't know it yet.

You think you really need
Some "magic wand"
To carry you to greatness

But no—you need only
To break your heart
With trying, with giving—
With teaching.

It takes a lifetime
To know it—
It finally takes
All you have

Until you cannot give any more
Because you finally know
That is what you need

It takes forever to comprehend
But that's okay,
You have a lifetime to understand
That this is what you want—no!
That this is what you need.

It Was Not Right to Love Him So Much
To my son, Mark (d. 2002)

I.
It was
Not good,
Even when he was a child
She knew it.
Such love should not be.

But he was sick. Puffed out little face,
Swollen cheeks that hid the slits
Of fevered eyes—
Every feature lost
To pain that claimed his smallness.

So she could not help the loving.
It flowed from a tormented heart
And a mother's fear
That death would come
And take her only child.

It hovered closely more than once.

The ice packs held the little body.
Tubes from clear glass bottles led to
Needles cruelly stabbed
In baby arms now limp from
The burden of their ordeal.

But worse, later on,
Years later,
When the sickness would not leave,
He would stand, barely, so sad it was,

He would stand caged in
By bars.
"Take me home, Mommy," he cried.
Shaking the crib
Until she could not bear his hurt.

But the words had burned themselves
In her young heart.
Too young she was for all of this,
A child herself really.

She heard them still—the words—
As the elevator rumbled to the ground
But did not silence the terrible pleas
Of the child who clenched the bars.

And she heard them later in the night,
And in the nights for years to come.

II.
No. it was not right to love him so much.
But there was the sickness.
So much, So often.

She was young, you know
And the suffering shocked her youth
So that she did the worst thing.
She loved him.

That love kept him
Her child-son
They were bonded and imprisoned by it.

That was not good,
His living was a miracle—we now know.
(His brother had no miracle.)
So he counted even more.

She spoiled him for this life.
Did too much.
Never wanted him unhappy again.
Silly woman, girl-child,

As though she could hold back
The catastrophes of living.

Petted him and picked him up;
Fed his dreams of mythic glory;
Fired his love of sports and books;
Fueled his imagination
And the quiet spirit of introspection
That grew inside of him.

Told him simply to "think and play."
Scant preparation for a world
That Wordsworth warned
Was …too much with us.

But, all right, she thought, she could
Fix the broken and beleaguered places.

Wrong! Too late.
She had filled him with too much already.
And he believed it,
Believed it because she taught it to him
And overdid the lesson.
He was too good a student.

He learned about life
From Edmund and Biff.
The theatre was a holy place.
Atticus and Walter Lee, too.

Mourned for Oppenheimer and JFK;
For the bad war, the forgotten causes,
And the Green Bay Packers.

III.
Thus, he flourished—strong and gentle,
With a kinship for the people.
What could she expect?

The child-son found his essence in
A foggy mixture of her foolish idealism
And neurotic passions.

He took it all.
Remembered most of it,
grew to his own size
And blended his dreams
With a love of justice
And an athlete's sense of fair play.

He made his mark,
Angry and confused sometimes
In a world that was not what she promised.
After all,
Atahualpa[1] did not rise!
Atahualpa did not rise!

No, it was not right
To love him so much,
Not good for either of them.
Both came to know it
And live with it—
A special secret they shared
That everyone knew.

---

[1] *In Peter Shaffer's play,* The Royal Hunt of the Sun, *Atahualpa, last prince of the Incas, put to death by Pisarro, claims immortality because he believed his father the Sun and his mother the Moon would raise him from the dead if his body was not mutilated. According to his wish, he was strangled by a cord. He does not rise.*

And even though it wasn't right,
It wasn't good,
She could not do it differently,
Not even if she had the chance again.

So they kept this agony between them.

Too late to change,
Too deep—too dear—too difficult.
And sometimes—sometimes,
Too unspeakably beautiful.

Her Lover's Landscape

"Don't leave me," she said.
In such a small voice
That no one heard
Except him.
And so he stayed.

He stayed to wash the wounds
And flush the fluids
And clear the fever
From the frail form
That called softly to him.

He stayed to swab
The organs when they swelled
And pack the cuts and carvings
With damp gauze, dripping wet
Pushed down hard so that skin bonded to skin.

No poetry there.
He said he loved her.
Just that.
So simple he never
Thought to say more
He just did what he did.
Because it had to be done.

Such love is not easy.
It asks everything of the giver.
And gives nothing back.
But sad sobbing murmurs of moist gratitude
For dirty work that no one likes or wants.

This is not loving, you say.
But the two know it is.

Not bodies clutching in sweaty passion.
Locking their loins in rocking rhythmic pleasures.
Exchanging sighs of ecstasy.
It's not like that.

Just small, daily
Dutiful acts:
The scrubbing, tending, cleaning up
Of disobedient bowels and bladder;
But tenderly done.
Oh, so tenderly that she hardly feels
The touch of those gnarled familiar hands
Rubbing her body—
Caressing the deepest
Caverns of womanhood
With unashamed love
That gives no ecstasy.

She had his children
And in the four decades of their life together
Much had passed between them.

But this was new.

The smell of sickness
Is not lovely.
It gives no fragrance
To love.
It is a foul, spoiled odor
Emitted from a tainted place.
The stained sheets, not from love's spilling,
But a rankness that
Forces flesh and gushes out.

No heavy, breathless panting there.

His manhood found
No home in her:
Not now,
Not ever, she thought.

Love is work.
Plain and simple.
A caretaker knows,
For she has been poked,
Picked, probed, prodded,
Needled, cut.

She took his gift inside her,
Lifted her head
From its troubles,
Anointed him with tears
And held him close,
Till their bodies did tingle
With the thrill of it.

And loved him—just that—
Loved him.
As though she had found
That missing part of herself
And could never let it go,
For surely she would
Split apart.

"So, hold on," he said.
And she did, once again,
As he told her;
As they made their way
To the rest of their lives,
Just "holding on."

Giving and getting
All the love they needed
Or could ever want.

For Melissa

Such beauty
Comes just once.
Not delicate
Not frail,

But strong—
A woman's strength
We knew
From the beginning.

She brought
Sunlight
And Laughter.

She brought down
The stars,
Glistened
From the start.

A roomful of dolls
Never called to her.
Doing was her name.

Yes! She made laughter.
So easily done.
Vibrant and alive

She was action.
Movement sublime.
Not like a butterfly
No!

Not delicate—
Not like that.
Just Lovely
Star crossed.

Dazzling,
Like a Bird in flight.
Yes! That was it.
A mother knows.

So people
Loved her.
Who could not?

She made her
Mark early,
Dominated the room—

Filled it with ideas
Beautiful clothes
And love in her heart
For people—
All people.

Everyone fell
Under her spell
Sought her
Loved her
And needed her.

She made things
Work!
That was her gift.

So, we loved her,
Just that!
Not enough
We sometimes
Thought
Not Enough
Not Enough

Sondra Shanen Melzer was born and raised in Stamford, Connecticut, where she taught high school English and drama for 40 years in the Stamford Public Schools. A graduate of the University of Connecticut, she earned her doctorate in English from New York University in 1984. After retiring from her position as teacher and English Department Head at Westhill High School, Stamford, she taught education, literature and women's studies courses at the University of Connecticut, Stamford, University of Bridgeport, and Sacred Heart University. She was named a faculty emerita at Sacred Heart in 2017.

A scholar of the novels of Philip Roth and the short stories of Dorothy Parker, she is the author of *Rhetoric of Rage*, a groundbreaking critical study of women in the writings of Parker. Dr. Melzer's writing has previously appeared in the National Council of Teachers of English publication *WILLA, The James Joyce Quarterly*, and in publications of Future 5, a program providing motivated under-resourced students in Stamford with the support and training to achieve their full potential as students, citizens, and future leaders.

Dr. Melzer lives with her husband Frank, an attorney, in Stamford, Connecticut.

www.ingramcontent.com/pod-product-compliance
Lightning Source LLC
Chambersburg PA
CBHW022126090426
42743CB00008B/1026